MY FIRST
Preschool
Shape Tracing
WORKBOOK

Copyright © 2024 by Callisto Publishing LLC
Cover and internal design © 2024 by Callisto Publishing LLC
Images by Shutterstock: © Chones: front cover, 33, back cover (balls); © Rvector: front cover, 63 (buttons); © Ekaterina Wolf: front cover, 37 (pizza); © chakkraphong jinthawet: front cover (hand); © Junjira Limcharoen: 7; © vvoe: 9 (branch); © Jaaak: 11 (dogs); © dwi putra stock: 13 (mouse); © Jr images: 15; © katarina_1: 17 (cloud); © djmilic: 19; © illustrator096: 21; © PSai2108: 23; © Tartila: 25 (cars); © Tatiana Popova: 25 (flag); © suns07butterfly : 27 (butterfly); © Lotus Images: 27 (flowers); © Evgeny Karandaev: 29 (train); © Tartila: 30; © P Maxwell Photography: 39; © johavel: 41, back cover (baseball diamond); © paniti Alapon: 45; © Vitalii Barida: 47; © Guzel Studio: 53, back cover (donut); © VectorPlotnikoff: 55; © Tartila: 57; © MooNoi_Amphol: 61; © CreatewithClaudia: 64; © Smit: 65; © Spreadthesign: 66; © nickfz: 67; © marinatiART: 69; © stockakia: 70; © pticelov: 72 (crayons); © KucherAV: 72, 73 (colored pencils, eraser, magnifying glass); © Mega Pixel: 73 (lunch box); © colors: 73 (highlighter); © Melica: 73 (watercolor set); © cammep: 78 (grass)
© Steve Mack: 5 (hand), throughout (border texture)
Getty Images: © paci77/iSt/DigitalVision Vectors: 9 (leaves); © D-Keine/iStock 13 (mouse hole); © Designer_things/iStock: 17 (puddle); © Nur Ataturk/iStock: 35 (car); © sadajiwa/iStock: 43 (spider); © LarisaBozhikova/DigitalVision Vectors: 59; © Michael Burrell/iStock: 72 (watercolor set)
Series Designer: Stephanie Mautone
Art Director: Carlos Esparza
Art Producer: Sue Bischofberger
Editor: Sasha Henriques
Production Editor: Nora Milman
Production Manager: Lanore Coloprisco

Callisto Publishing and the colophon are registered trademarks of Callisto Publishing LLC

Published by Callisto Publishing LLC C/O Sourcebooks LLC
P.O. Box 4410, Naperville, Illinois 60567-4410
(630) 961-3900
callistopublishing.com

This product conforms to all applicable CPSC and CPSIA standards.

Source of Production: 1010 Printing Asia Unlimited, Kwun Tong, Hong Kong, China
Date of Production: November 2023
Run Number: 5034870

Printed and bound in China.
OGP 10 9 8 7 6 5 4 3 2 1

MY FIRST Preschool Shape Tracing WORKBOOK

Fun Activities to Teach Pencil Control *and* Pre-Writing Skills

SARAH CHESWORTH

callisto publishing
an imprint of Sourcebooks

Note to Caregivers

This book was created to help your child develop the fine motor skills needed for writing and give them fun opportunities to practice pen control. As a parent and teacher, I know that the pre-writing skills taught in this workbook will give your child a strong foundation and confidence as they begin learning to write.

First, your child will practice simple strokes and line tracing. Next, they will practice tracing shapes and creating simple pictures. Here are a few tips to ensure your child gets the most from this workbook:

- I recommend having your child complete this workbook using a thin marker. Pencils can cause unnecessary frustration for children learning to write, because they don't write smoothly and the lead breaks easily.

- This book has been divided into sections. At the beginning of each section, you will find a brief introduction and directions for guiding your child through that section.

- Take your time working through this book. Children learn at different speeds, and little learners may need multiple sessions to complete each page. Take breaks as needed and keep learning a fun and positive experience!

- After your child is able to trace the lines and shapes in this book, encourage them to draw them freehand.

Enjoy this special time learning with your child!

Pen Control Practice and Tracing Lines

Tracing lines is a great way for your child to develop and practice pen control. In this section, they will practice tracing different types of dotted lines. Learning these strokes will help your child write uppercase and lowercase letters when they are ready.

First, your child will practice tracing each dotted line. A dot will show where to begin and an arrow will guide their stroke. Then they will practice tracing that type of line with a fun activity. If your child is able, encourage them to use a proper writing utensil grip as they complete these pages.

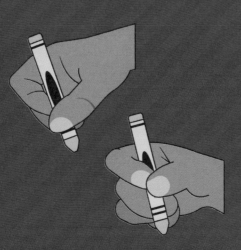

Trace each line.
Start at the dot and follow the arrow.

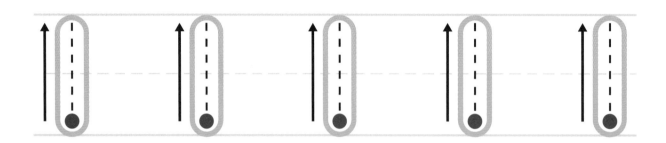

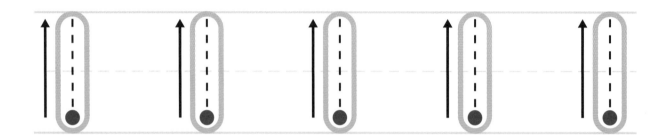

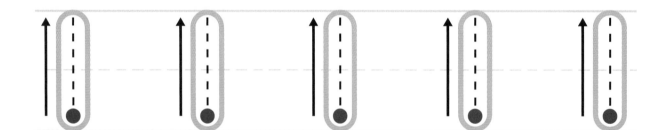

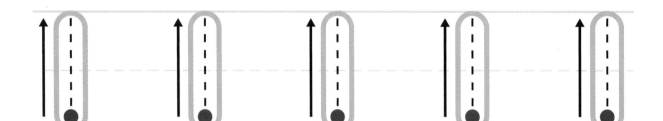

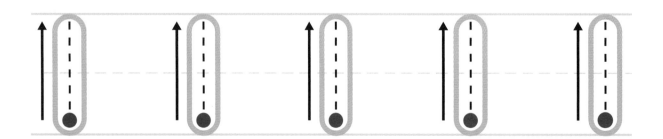

Trace each dotted line to complete the buildings.

Trace each line. Start at the dot and follow the arrow.

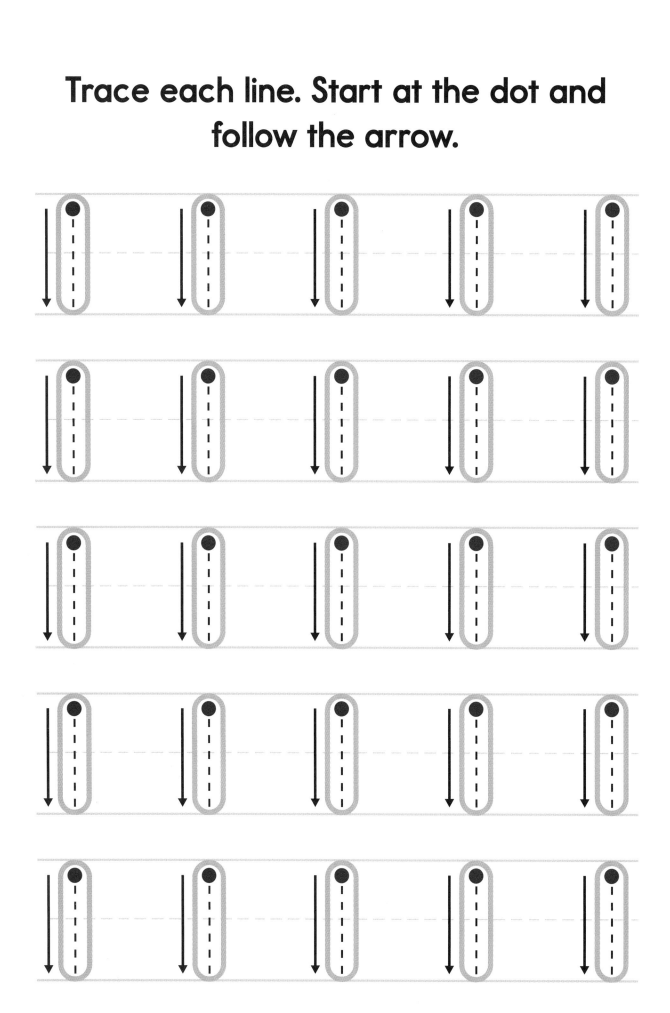

Trace each dotted line. Start at the branch and trace to the leaf below.

Trace each line. Start at the dot and follow the arrow.

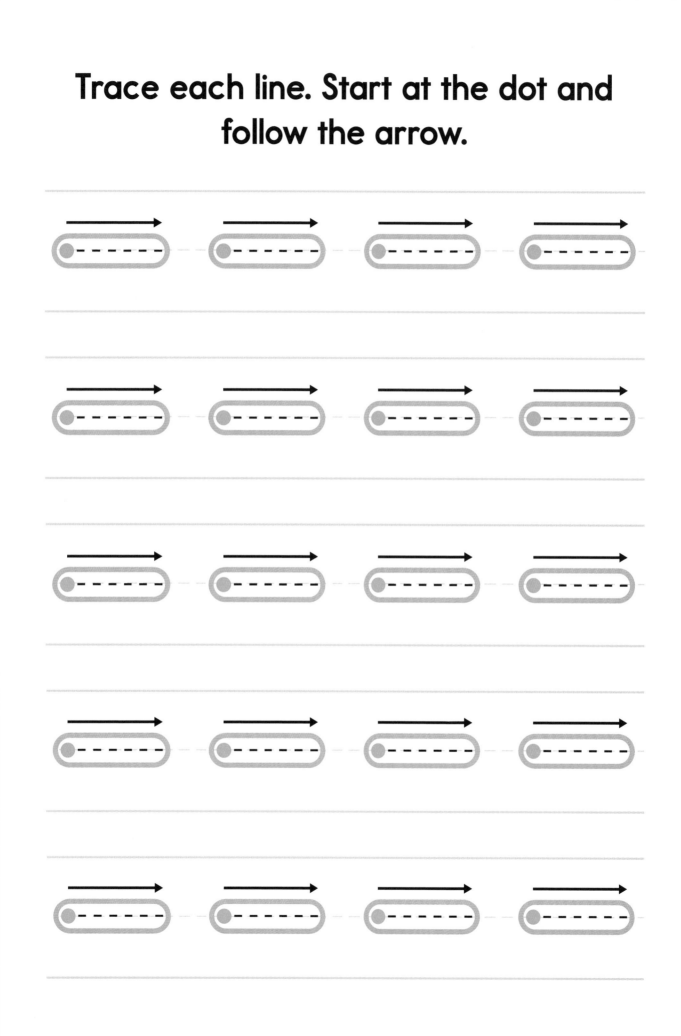

Start at the dog and trace the line to its bowl.

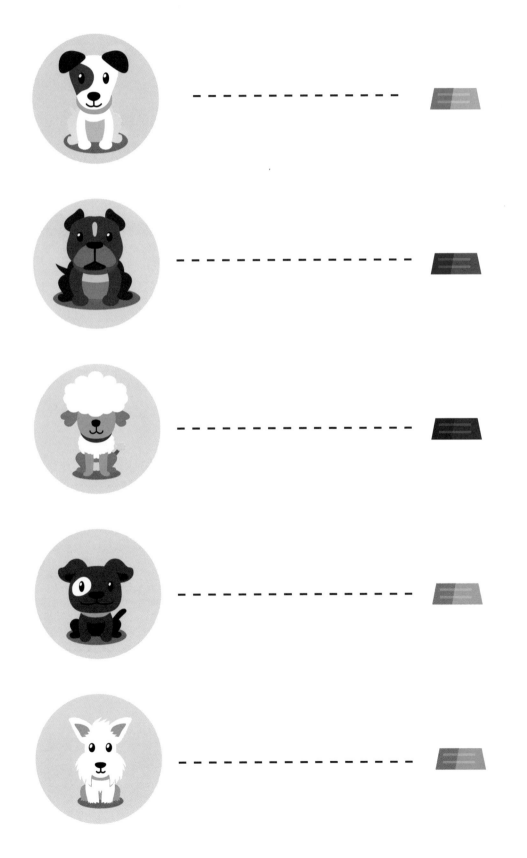

Trace each line. Start at the dot and follow the arrow.

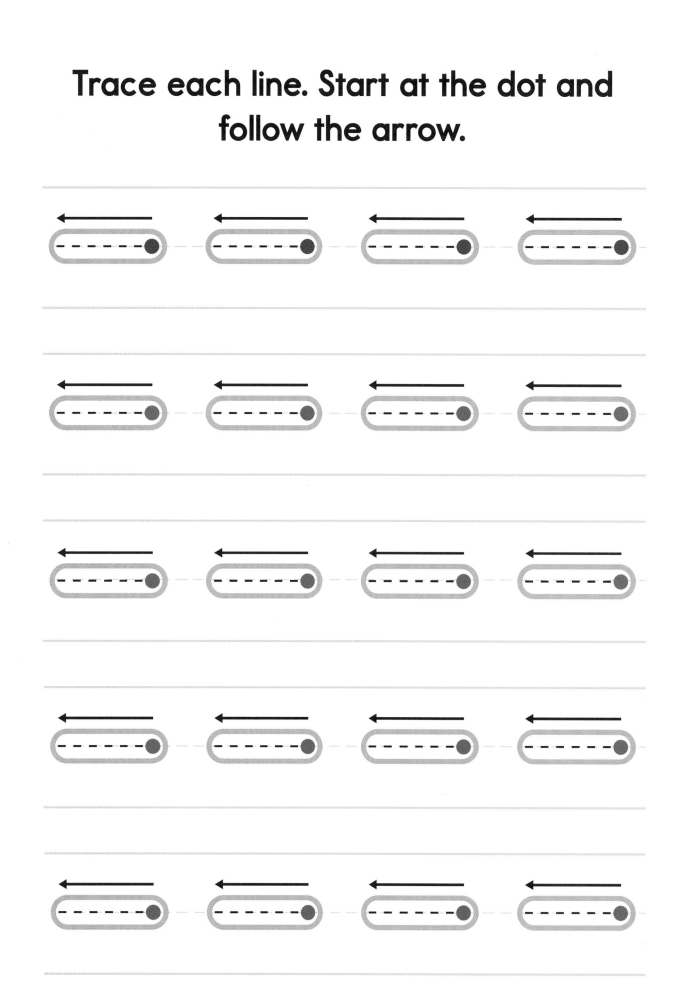

Start at the mouse and trace the line back to its hole.

 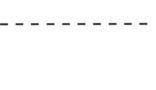 

Trace each line. Start at the dot and follow the arrows.

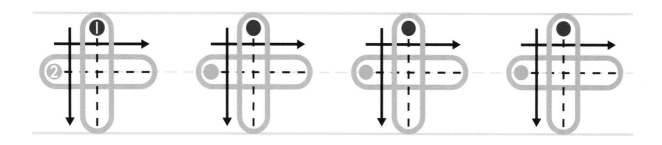

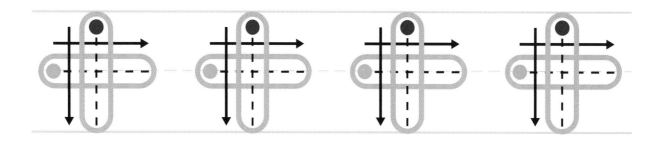

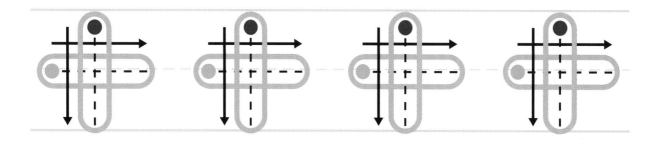

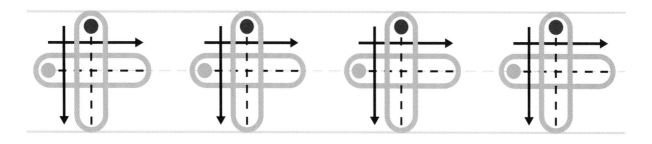

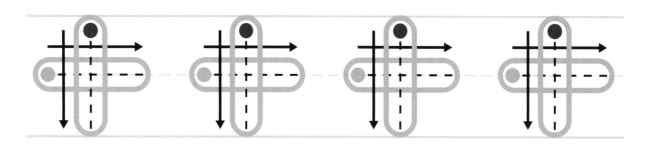

Trace each line to complete the waffle.

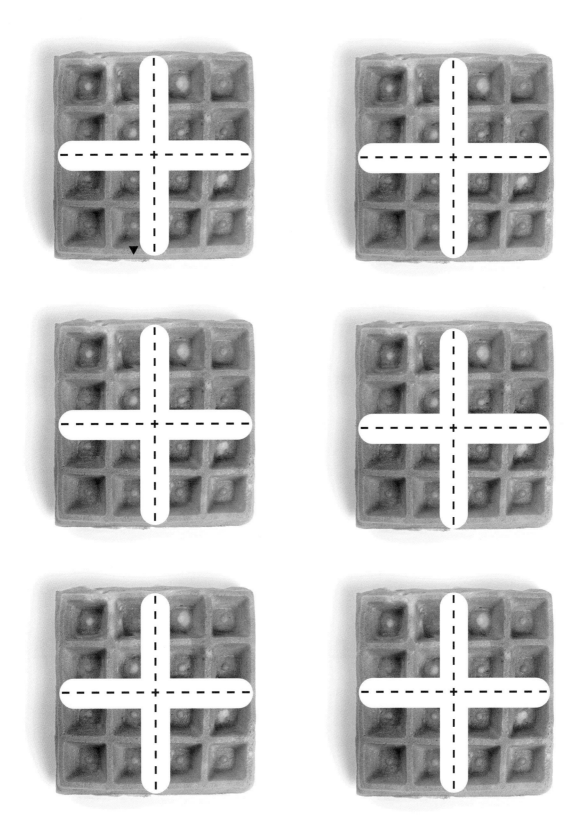

Trace each line. Start at the dot and follow the arrow.

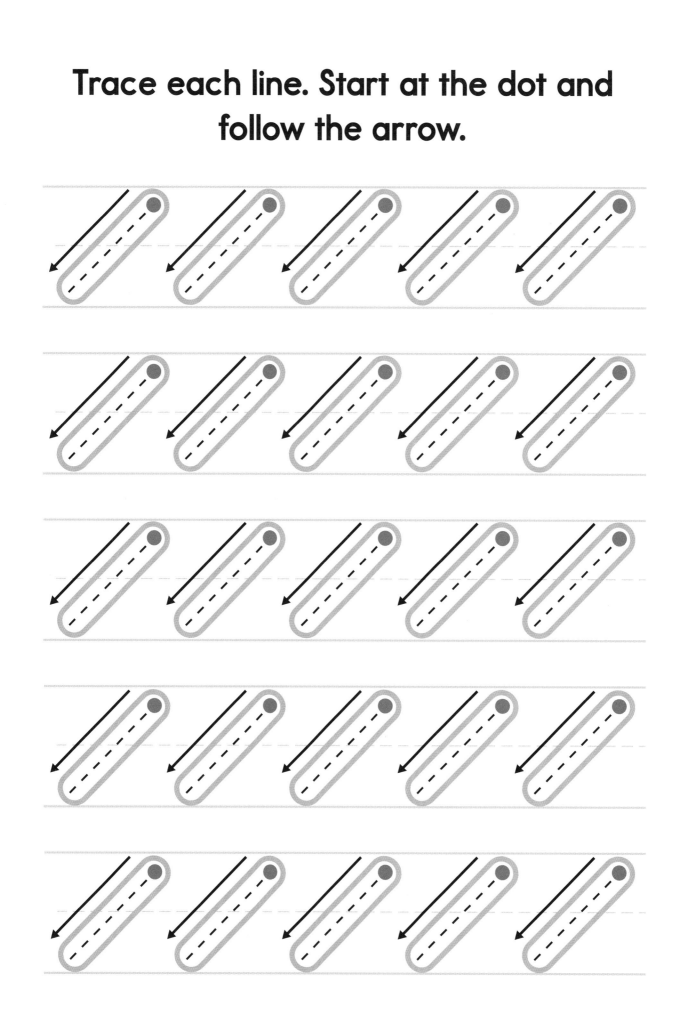

Trace each line of rain.

Start at the dot. Follow the arrow and trace the dotted line.

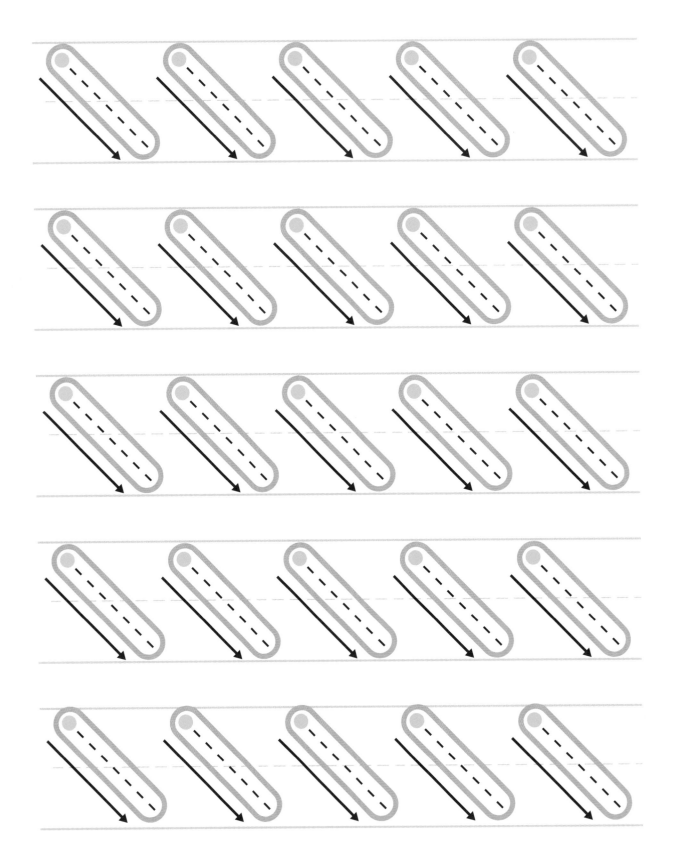

Start at the top of the slide and trace the line down.

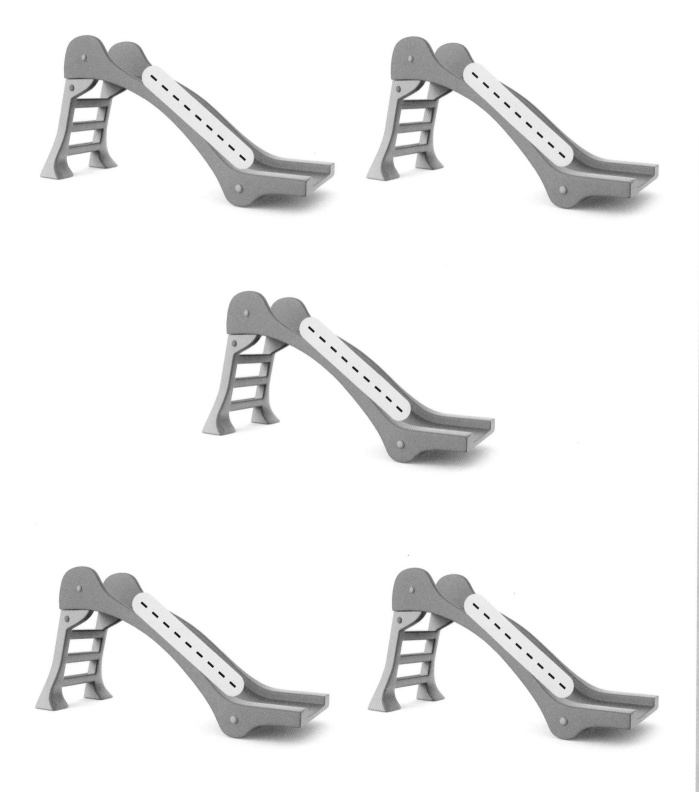

Trace each line. Start at the dot and follow the arrows.

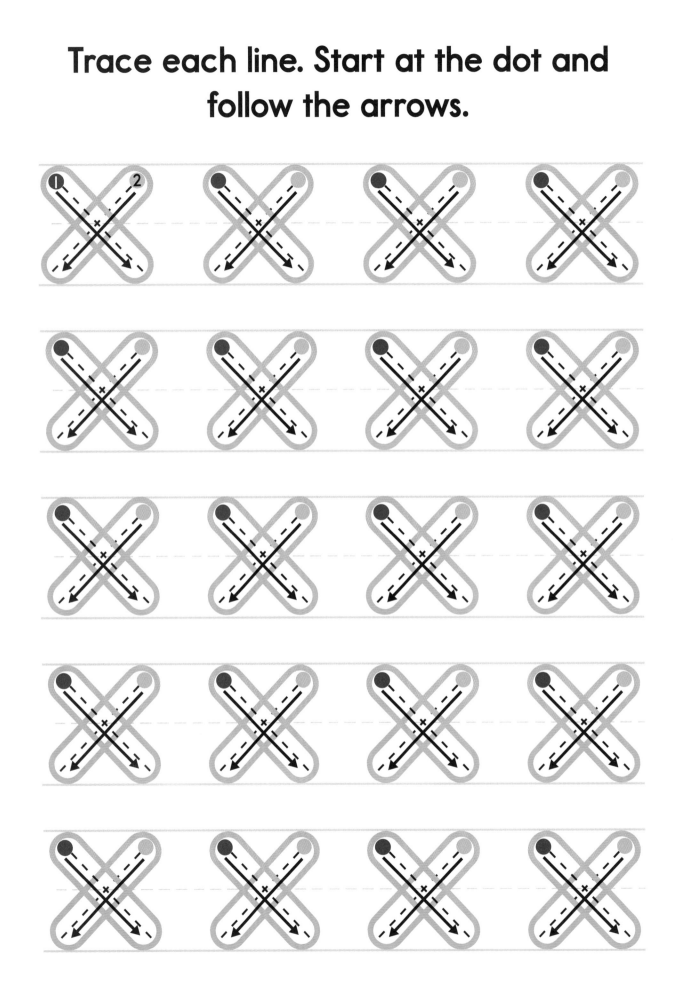

Trace each X to mark the treasure.

 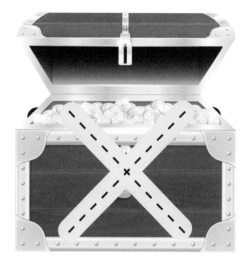

 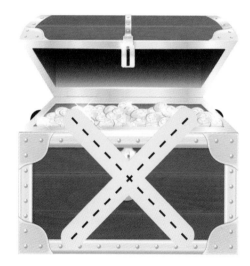

Trace each line. Start at the dot and follow the arrows.

Trace each line to make the alligator's teeth.

Trace each line. Start at the dot and follow the arrow.

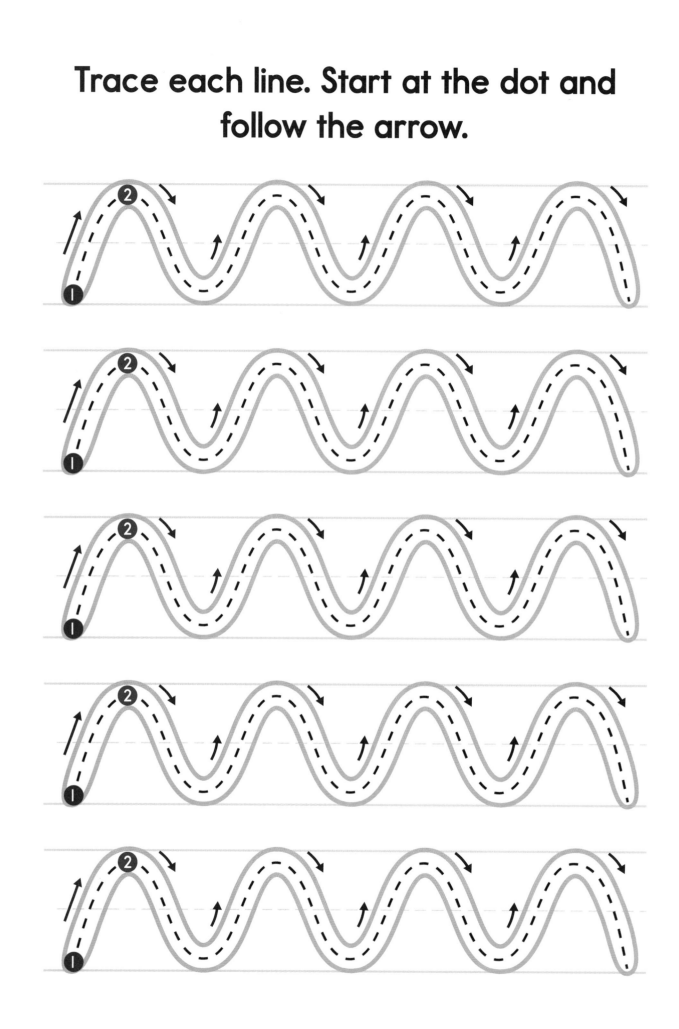

Trace the line to lead each car to the finish line.

Start at the dot. Follow the arrow and trace the dotted line.

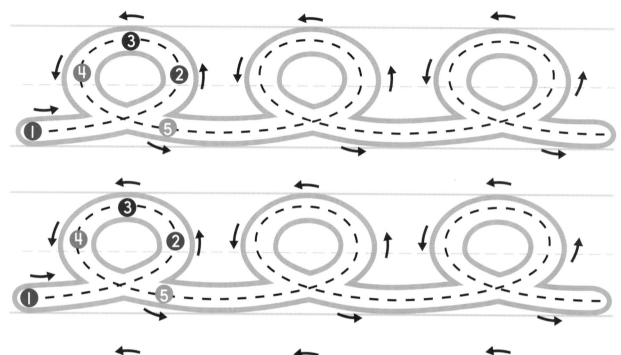

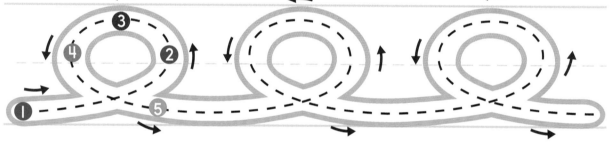

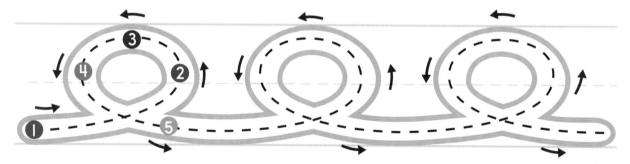

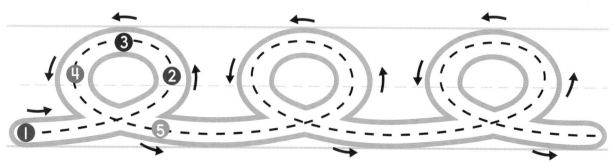

Trace the line to lead the butterfly to the flowers.

Trace the lines. Start at the dot and follow the arrows.

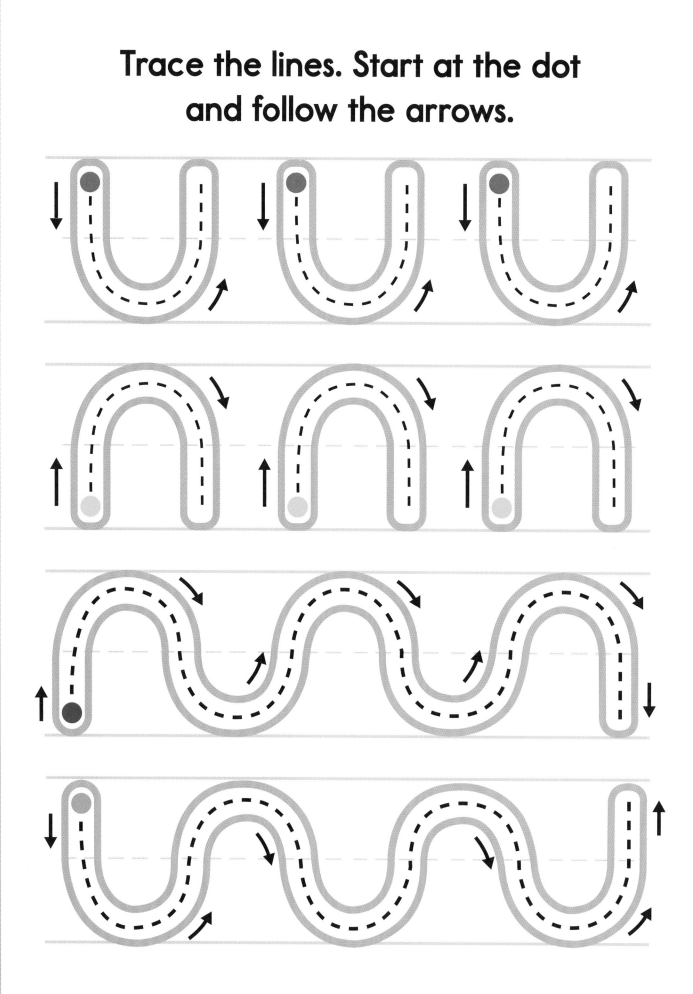

Trace the lines from the trains to the shape that matches the shape on each train car.

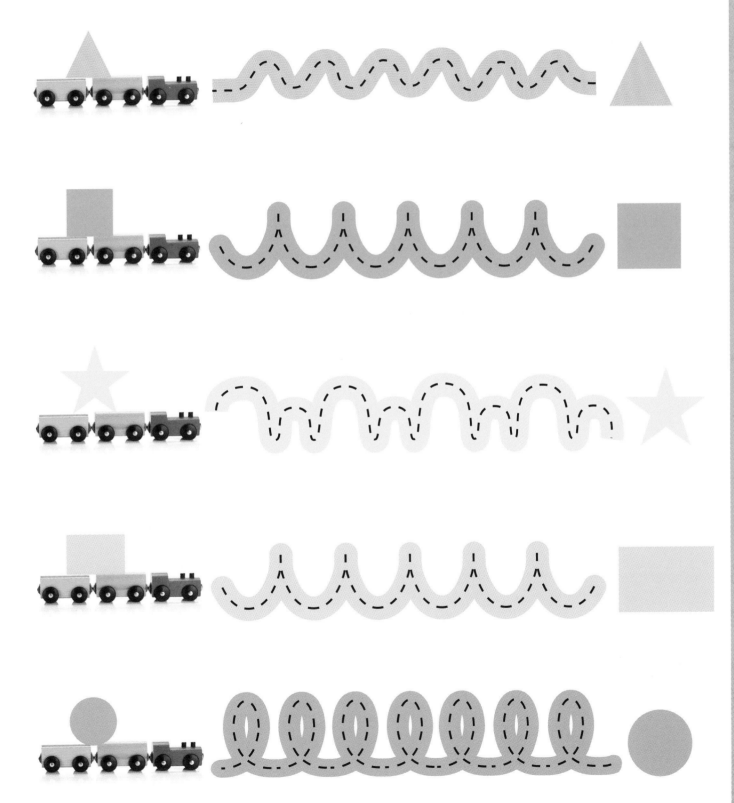

Trace each line to connect the matching pair of socks.

Shape Tracing

● ▲ ■ ▼ ● ● ▲ ■ ▼ ● ● ▲ ■ ▼ ● ● ▲ ■

Now that your child has practiced tracing lines, they are ready to begin tracing shapes. In this section, your child will practice tracing different types of shapes.

First, your child will be tracing dotted lines to form various shapes. A dot will show them where to begin and an arrow will guide their strokes. Then they will practice tracing that shape with a fun activity. Finally, they will trace pictures with multiple types of lines and shapes! If your child is able, encourage them to use a proper writing utensil grip as they complete these pages.

Start at the dot. Follow the arrow and trace the dotted line.

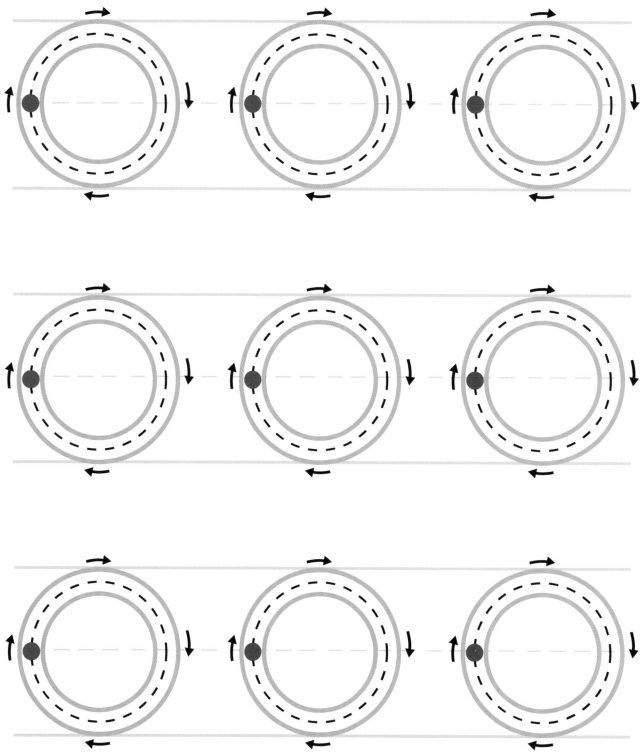

Trace each circular ball.

Start at the dot. Follow the arrow and trace the dotted line.

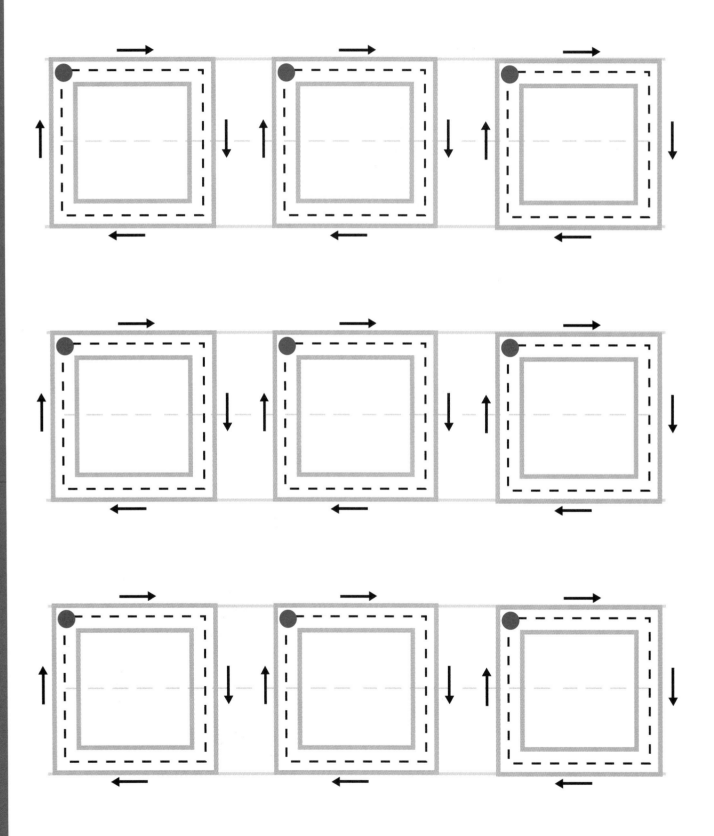

Trace each square in the racing flag.

Start at the dot. Follow the arrow and trace the dotted line.

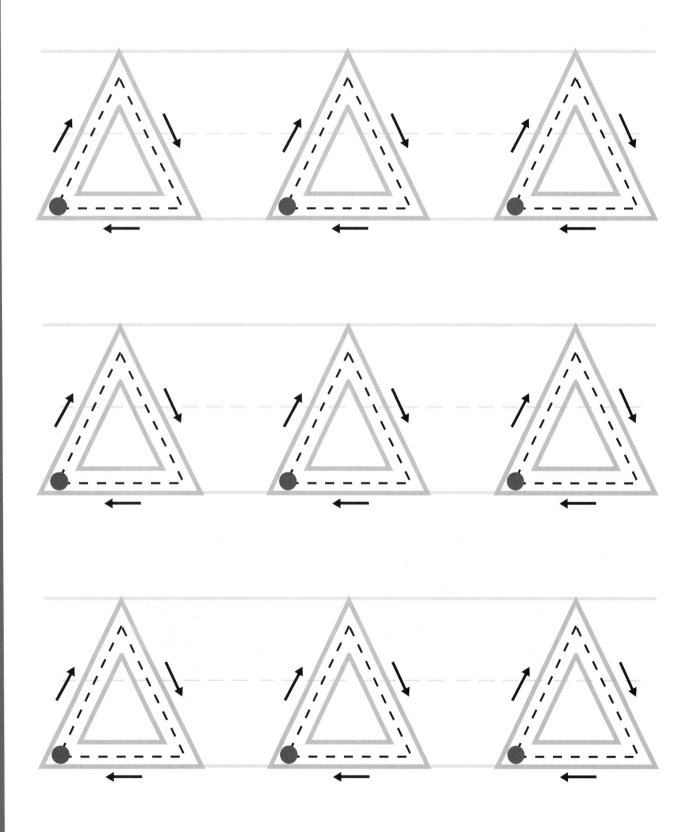

Trace each triangular slice of pizza.

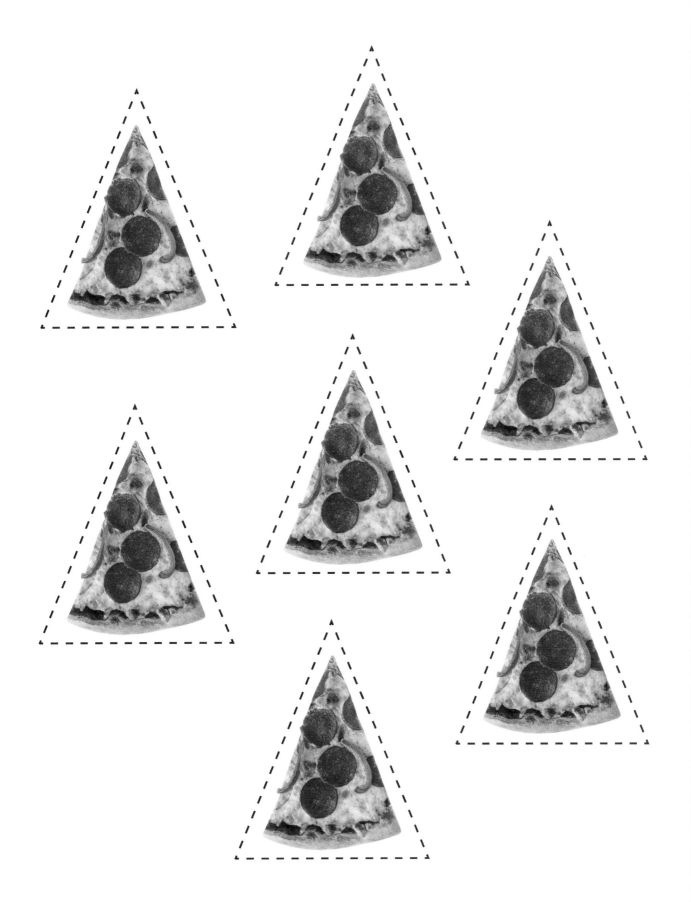

Start at the dot. Follow the arrow and trace the dotted line.

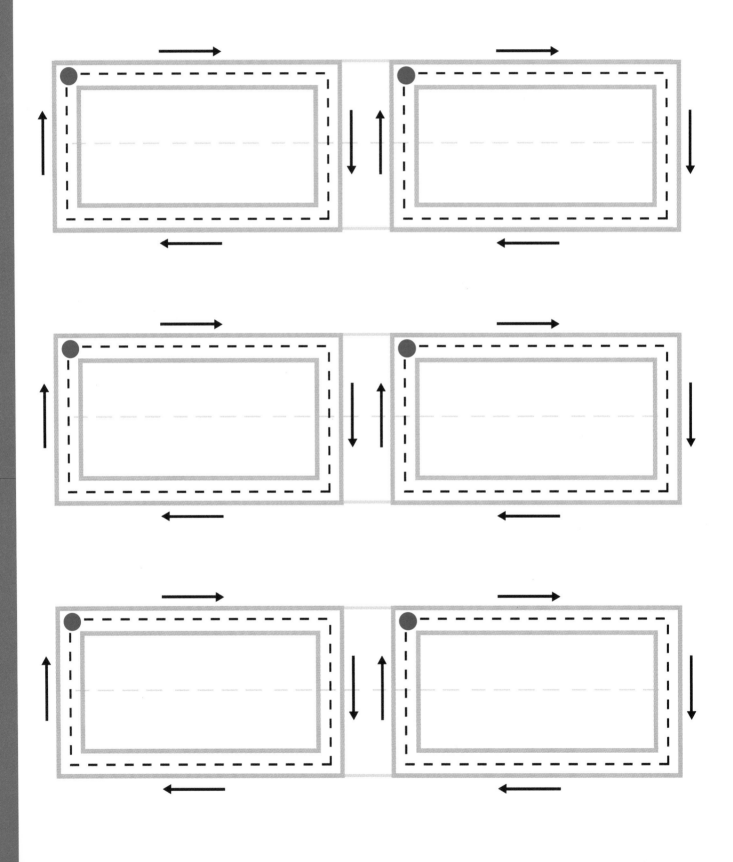

Trace each rectangular candy bar.

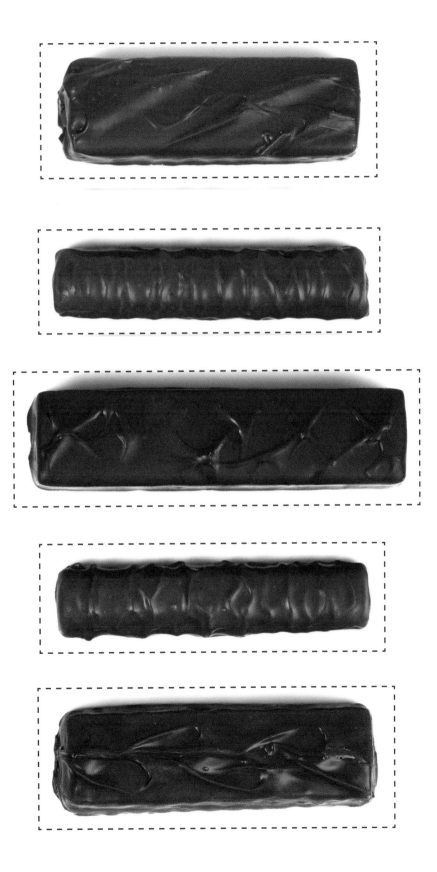

Start at the dot. Follow the arrow and trace the dotted line.

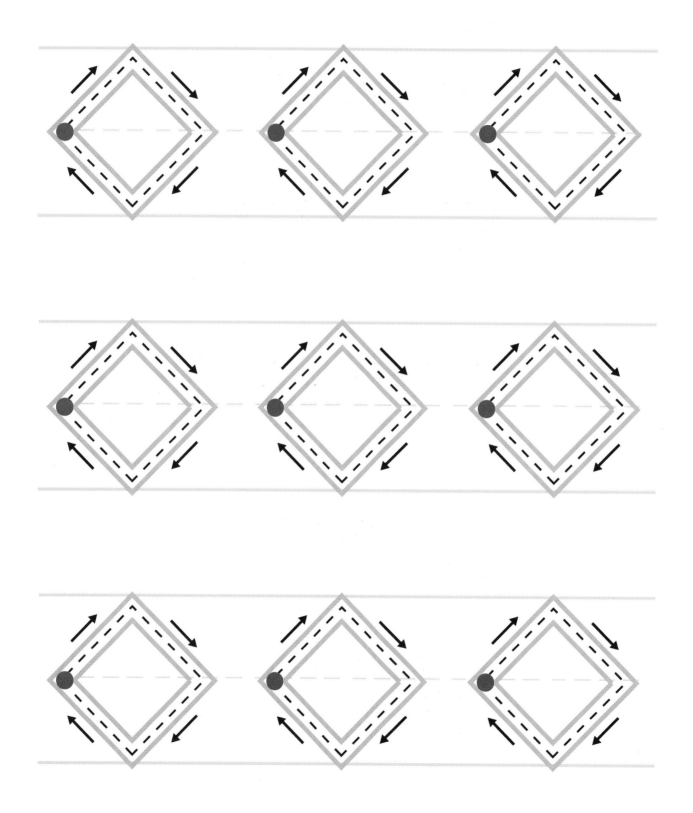

Trace each diamond on the baseball field.

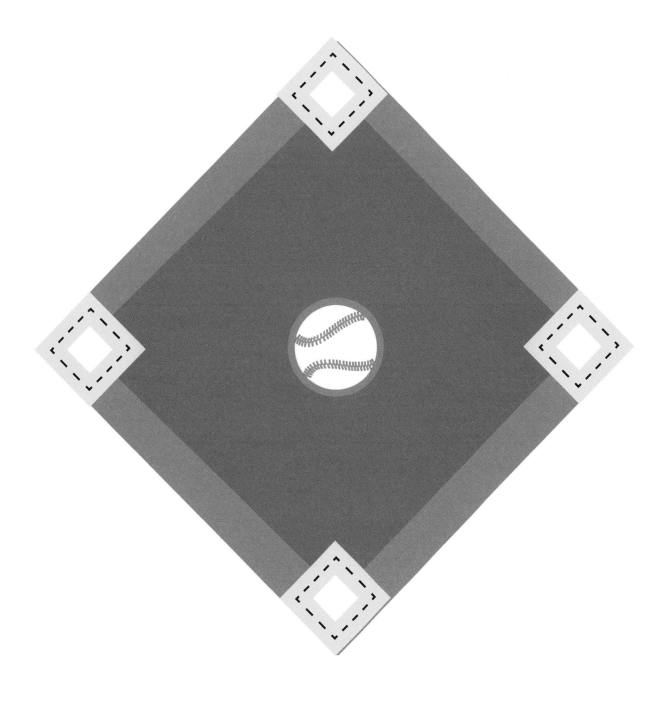

Start at the dot. Follow the arrow and trace the dotted line.

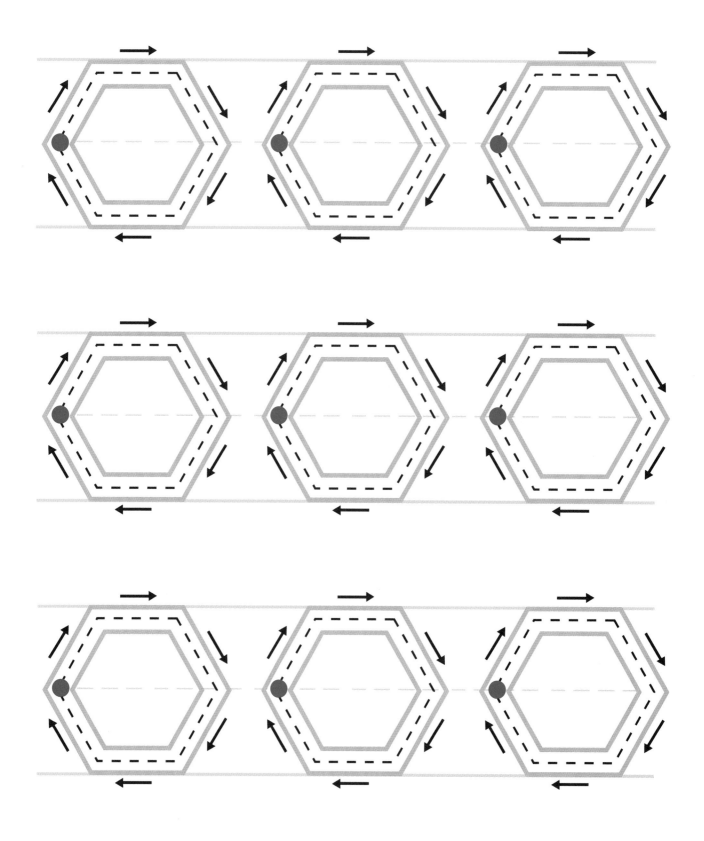

Trace each hexagon in the web.

Start at the dot. Follow the arrow and trace the dotted line.

Trace each white star in the night sky.

Start at the dot. Follow the arrow and trace the dotted line.

Trace each heart on the bug.

Start at the dot. Follow the arrow and trace each dotted line.

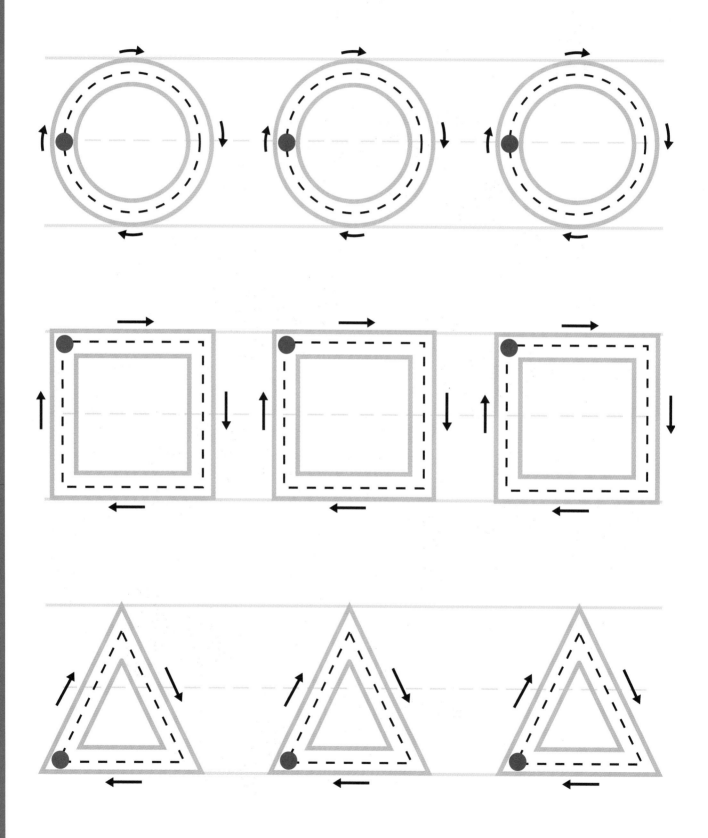

Start at the dot. Follow the arrow and trace each dotted line.

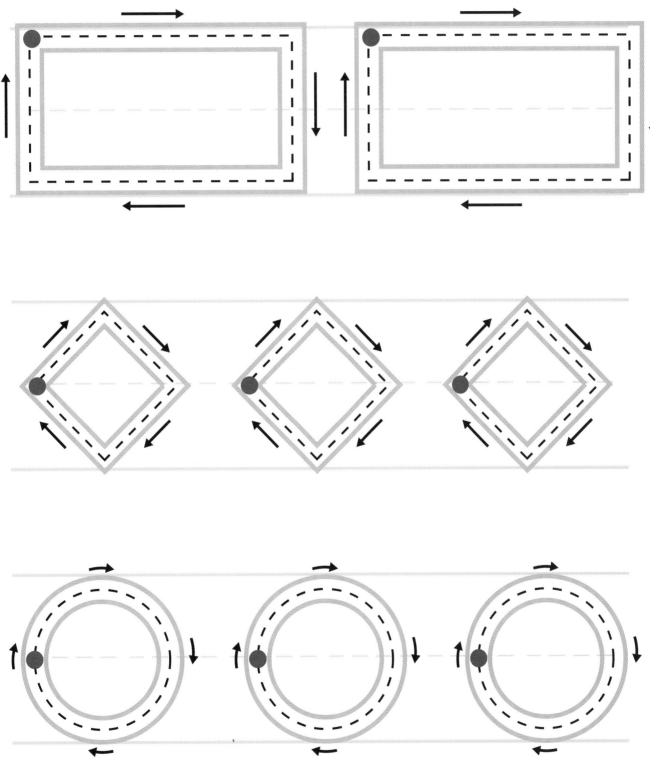

Start at the dot. Follow the arrow and trace each dotted line.

Shape and Line Combination Tracing Practice

●▲■▼▼●□■●▲■▼▼●□■●▲■▼▼●□■●▲■

In this final section of the book, your child will practice tracing different shapes and lines together to create pictures! First, they will review how to trace the lines and shapes. A dot will show them where to begin tracing each shape, and an arrow will guide their strokes. Then they will practice tracing different lines and shapes together in one picture! If your child is able, encourage them to name each shape that they trace and use a proper writing utensil grip as they complete these pages.

Trace each line and shape.

Trace the donut and sprinkles.
What shape do you see?

Trace each shape.

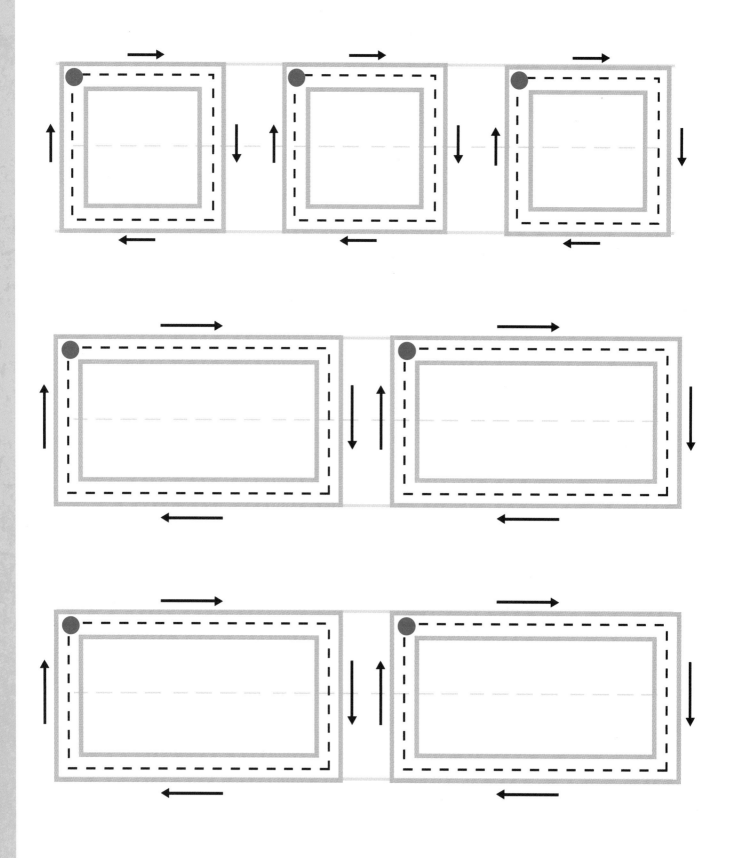

Trace each gift.
What shapes do you see?

Trace each shape and line.

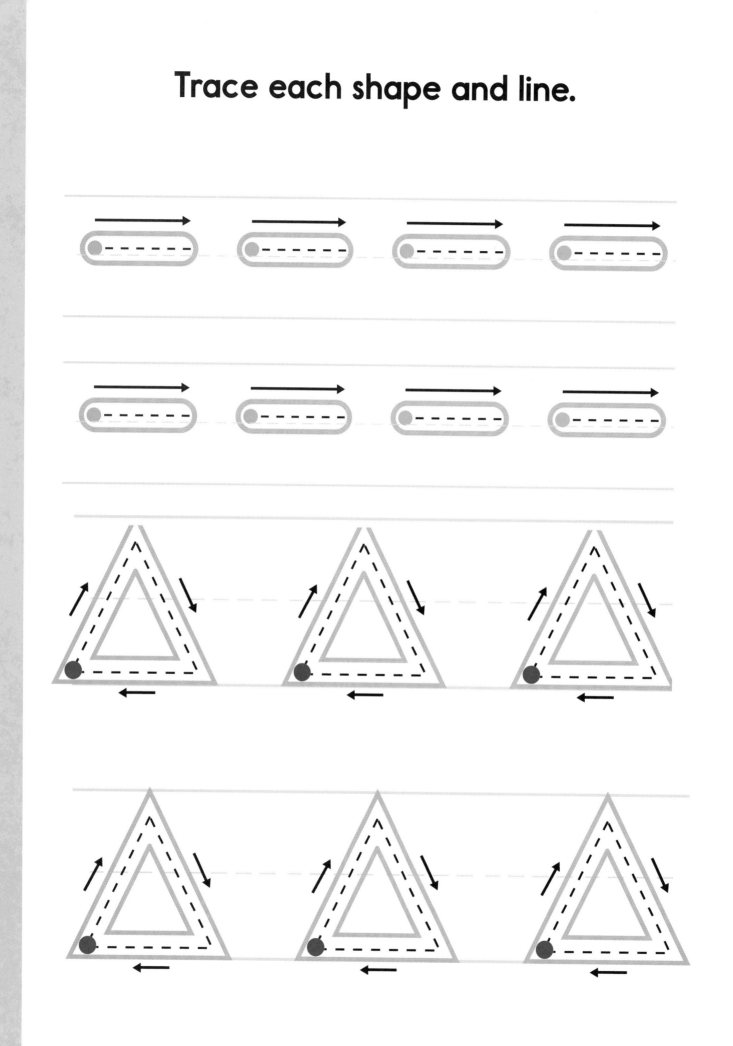

Trace the party hat.
What shapes do you see?

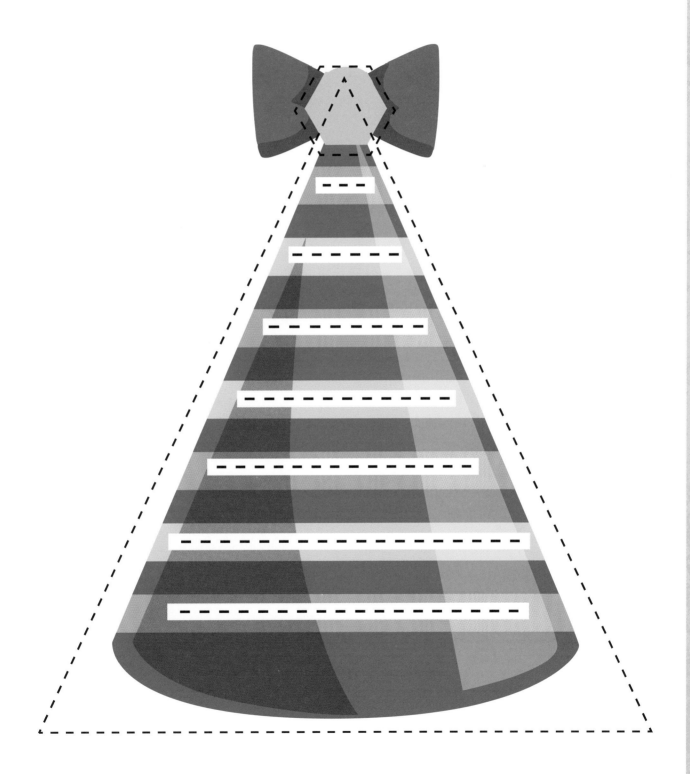

Trace each shape and line.

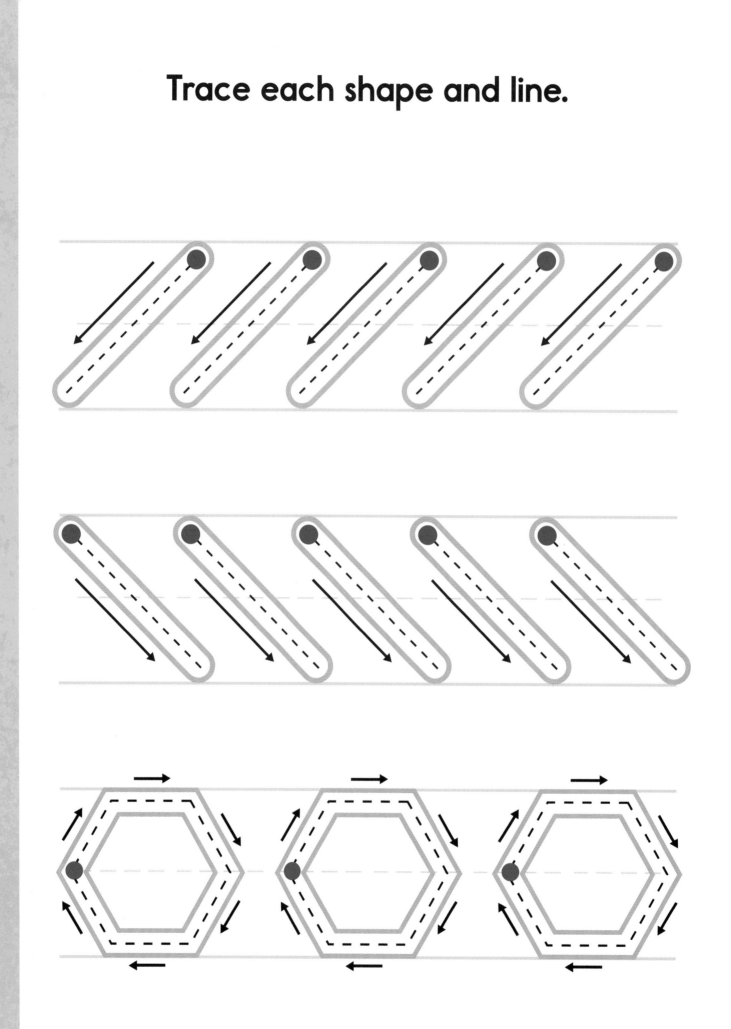

Trace each honeycomb.
What shape do you see?

Trace each line and shape.

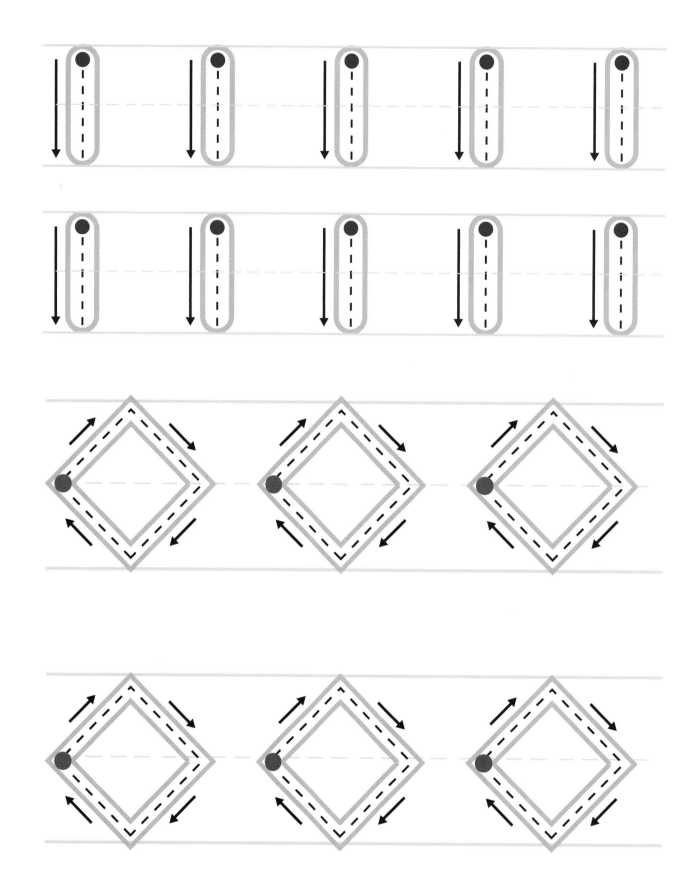

Trace each sign and pole.
What shape do you see?

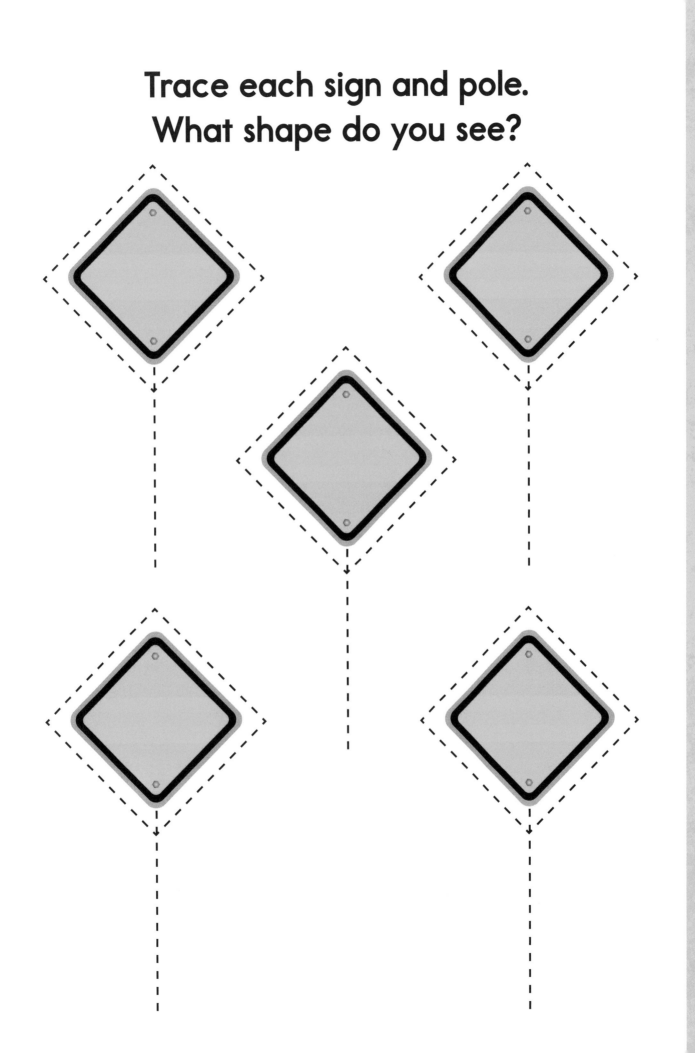

Trace each shape.

Trace each button.
What shapes do you see?

Trace each shape to complete the quilt.
What shapes do you see?

Trace each shape on the xylophone.
What shapes do you see?

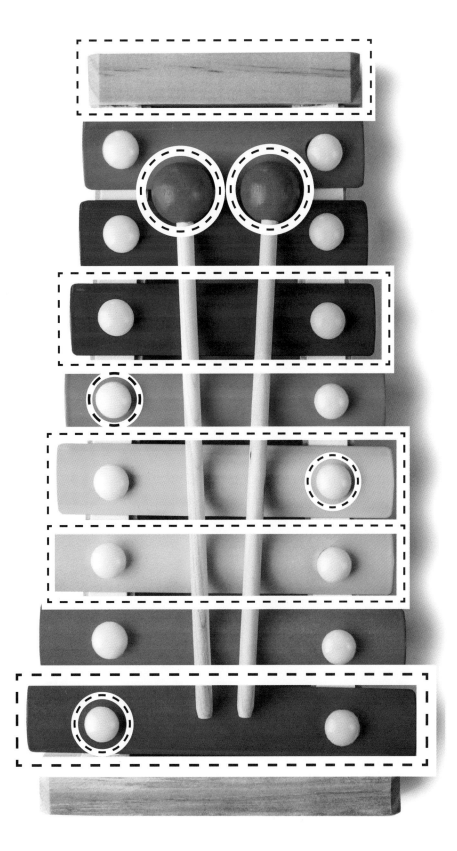

Trace each line and shape to complete the butterfly. What shapes do you see?

Trace each shape to complete the house. What shapes do you see?

Trace each shape to complete the train.
What shapes do you see?

Trace each shape to complete the mouse. What shapes do you see?

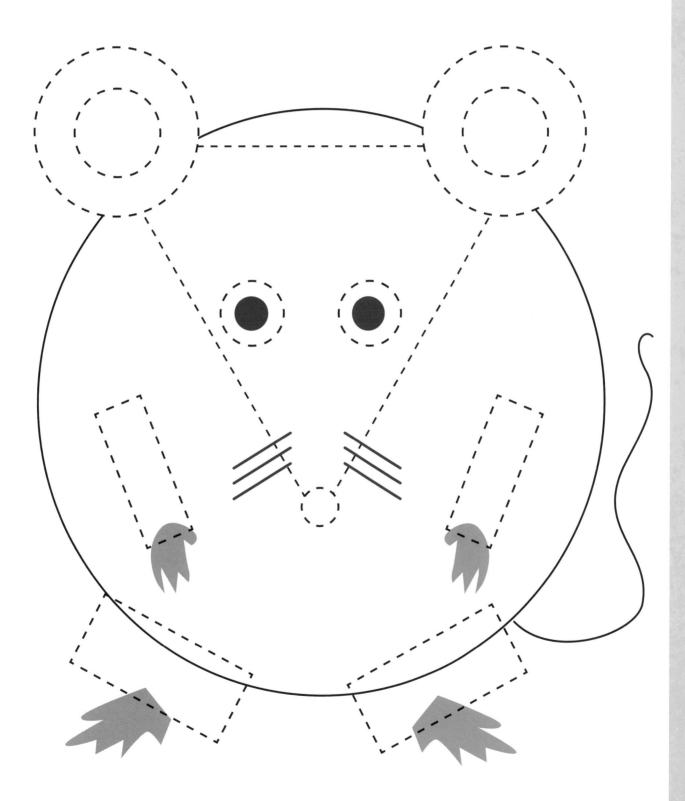

Trace each kite and string.
What shapes do you see?

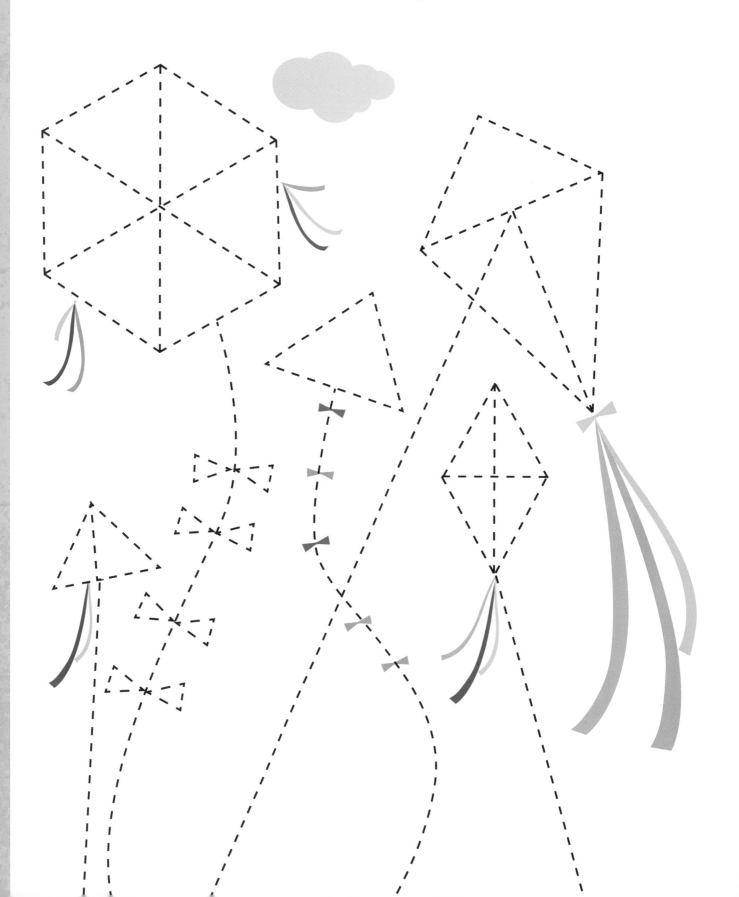

Trace each shape to complete the fish.
What shapes do you see?

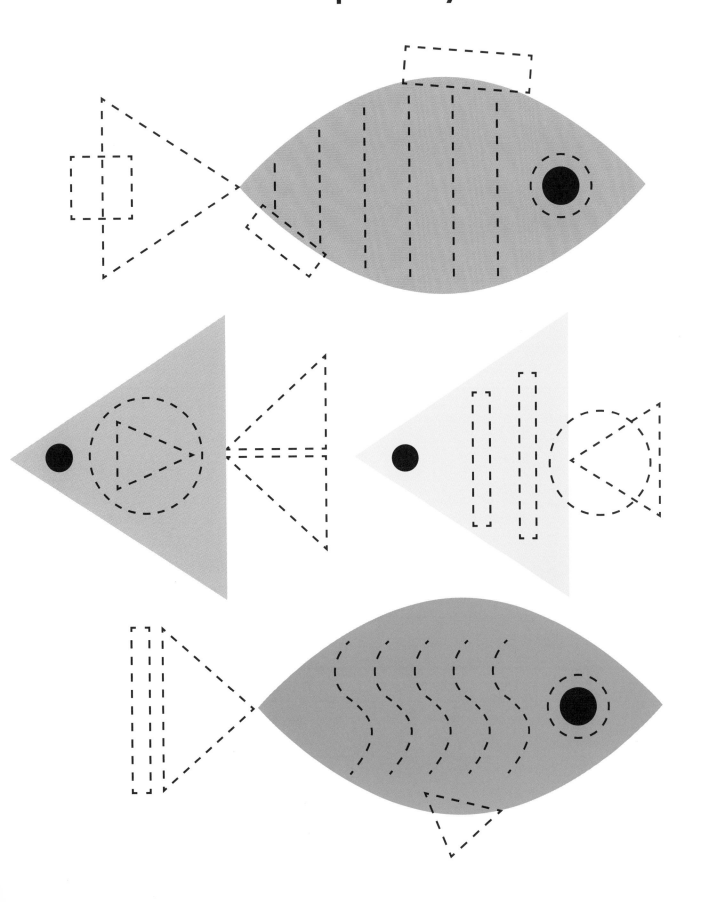

Trace each line and shape.
What shapes do you see?

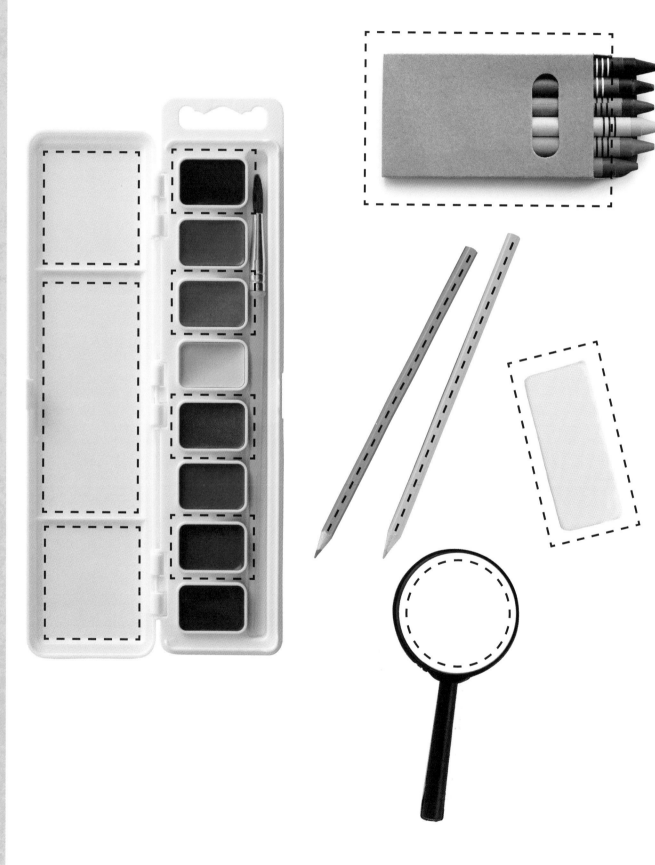

Trace each line and shape.
What shapes do you see?

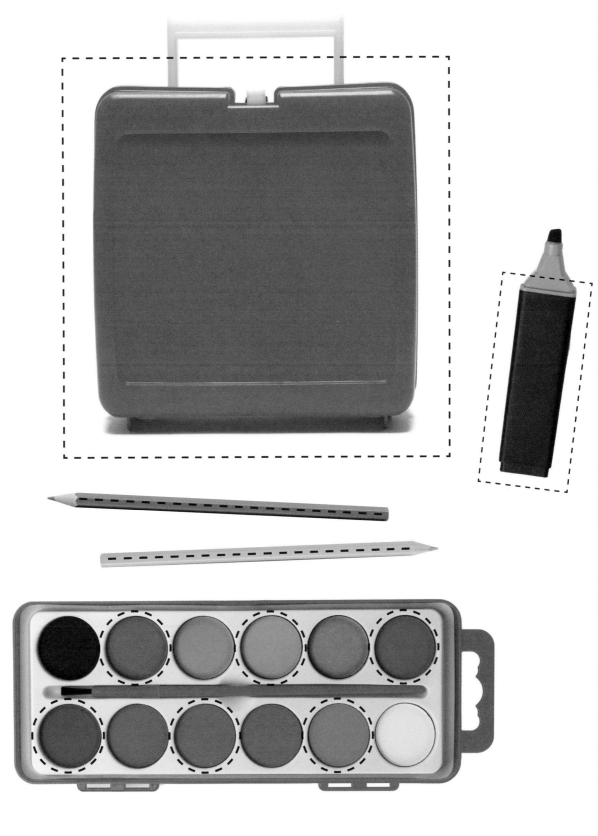

Trace each shape. Take your time.

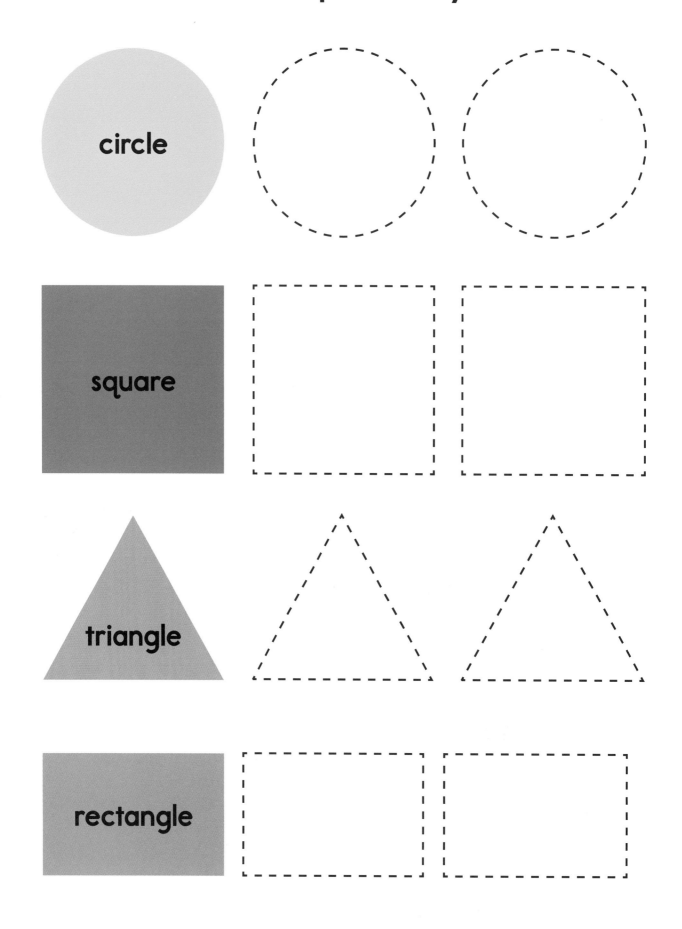

circle

square

triangle

rectangle

Trace each shape. Take your time.

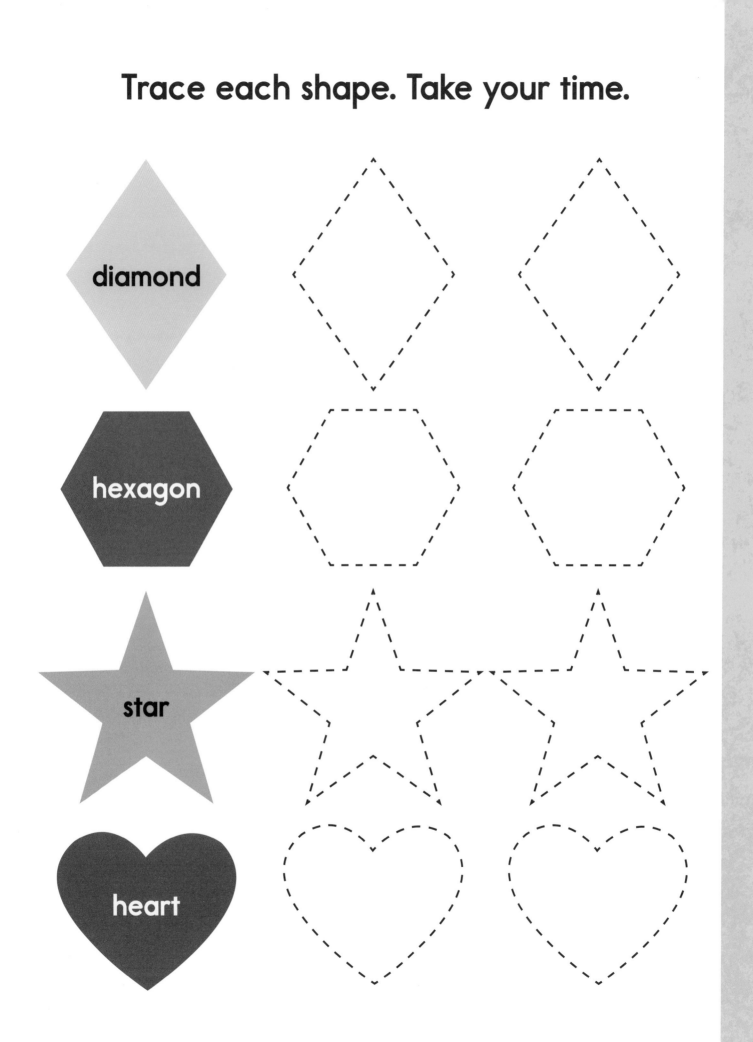

Trace each of the shapes that you have learned!

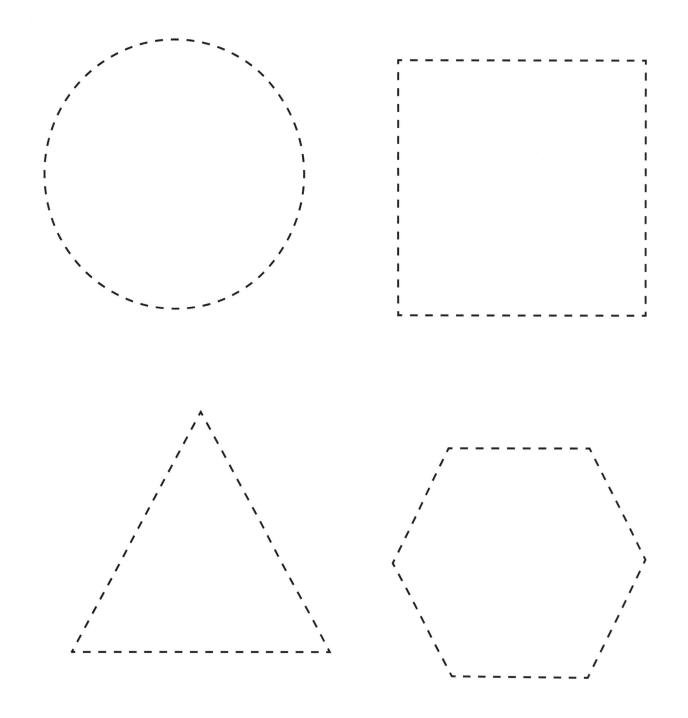

Trace each shape to make a rocket. Then color the picture. 3, 2, 1, blast off!

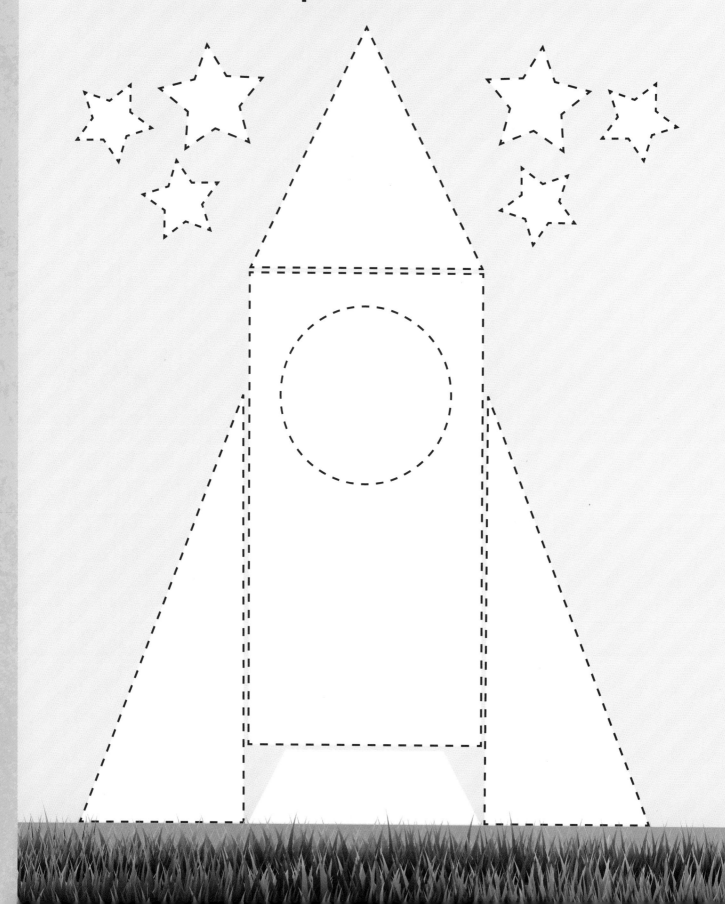

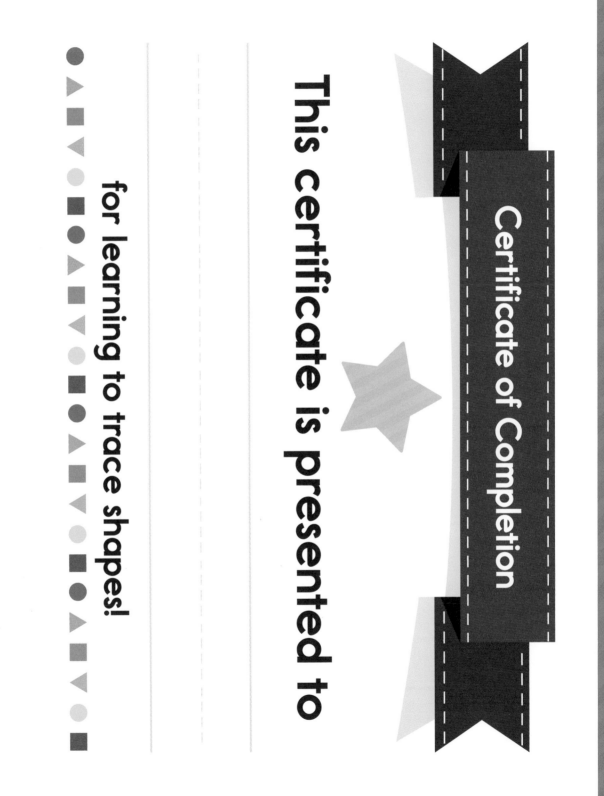

Certificate of Completion

This certificate is presented to

for learning to trace shapes!

Date _____

About the Author

 **Sarah Chesworth** is a former kindergarten and first grade teacher. Now she spends her days teaching her own two little girls. She also helps busy parents and teachers make learning fun through her website and online teaching resources. She holds a bachelor's degree in early childhood education from Texas Tech University.